More Than A Parachute

More Than A Parachute

A Personal Poetic Response
To The Apostles' Creed

James L. Mayfield

RESOURCE *Publications* • Eugene, Oregon

MORE THAN A PARACHUTE
A Personal Poetic Response To The Apostles' Creed

Resource Publications
An Imprint of Wipf and Stock Publishers
199 W. 8th Ave., Suite 3
Eugene, OR 97401

www.wipfandstock.com

PAPERBACK ISBN: 978-1-5326-7548-5
HARDCOVER ISBN: 978-1-5326-7549-2
EBOOK ISBN: 978-1-5326-7550-8

Manufactured in the U.S.A.   MARCH 8, 2019

This book is dedicated to

Rita Browning Mayfield
my dear wife and my best friend.

She was God's special gift of grace
to all who were blessed to know her.

Contents

CONTENTS

CONTENTS

Contents

Preface

HOW THESE PERSONAL RESPONSES CAME INTO BEING:
From time to time across the years I have used The Apostles' Creed as a catalyst for my personal meditation. Of course, I have also read and thought about comments by others regarding the history of this creed and the theological implications in this creed, but the heart of my spiritual exercise has been to try to put in my words what I was discovering about the Gospel, life in general and my life in particular as I meditated on the words and phrases in this ancient affirmation of faith. In the process of writing I found myself using language more like a poet than like an academic theologian or historian. Across the years as my experience expanded and my insight deepened, I have revised and added to the poetic reflections in this little book.

The result is this book is not an attempt to educate the reader regarding the historic background of this creed, nor is this collection of poetic responses an attempt to give a theological analysis of the creed. What I have written is a very personal witness of faith rather than an academic theological or historical exposition.

For those readers who are interested in a little more background information about creeds in general and this creed in partiular, I have added a short article to the end of this volume: "Comments About Creeds In General And The Apostles' Creed In Particular." Some readers may find it helpful to read this background information first.

I have also included the title of a few books I think can be helpful to someone who is just beginning to be curious about the history of The Apostles' Creed and what influences have shaped its content across the years.

A suggestion regarding the reading of these reflections:

Most of us speed read; this is to say we read much faster than we speak or listen. As is true of reading poems, these poetic reflections are best read at the slower rate of listening so the reader can hear or imagine the inflections that give vitality to the words.

JIM MAYFIELD

Background

THE PRIMAL TRAGEDY

(See John 1:1 and Genesis 2:4-3:24.)

Long centuries and centuries
before there was an Abraham,
before there was an Ur to leave,
a time when human critters lived
in caves and had no words
to use in thinking or in talk,
a human critter looked up, saw
in awe the stars and wondered "Why?"
although he had no words to think
or speak the "Why?" that filled his mind.

Across long centuries the sounds,
that humans made around the fire
were given meaning and became
much more, much more than merely noise,
much more than words to use in speech;
the sounds became words to mean
"stick" or "hungry" or "fire"
"death" or "fear" or "hope"
became beginning tools we humans use
in thinking and talking about "Why?"
when we are awestruck by the stars
or wondering what happens to
each one of us when we are dead.

Around the nighttime fire they sat
using words to entertain with stories
and discovering in the tales they told
much more than fireside entertainment.
To their surprise they glimpsed the truth
that's so much more than mere facts.
Surprised they sensed a meaning that
was more than words alone can say.
They sensed Whatever is behind
the everything that was or is
or will be was using the words they made,
to speak the Word beyond their words.

Mistaking their words for the Word,
their confidence expanded and with pride
their awe turned into human arrogance.
With unconscious pride they believed
their words spoke the Word so true
they rejected any disagreement.
They knew it all—just as the snake had promised.
And now like them we think in time
with computing help we too will know it all.
Whether we believe in God or not
we find ourselves inside the tale
of Eve and Adam suckered by that snake
and losing more much more than innocence.
In arrogance and pride we lose our way.

"I believe . . ."

MY JOURNEY TO BELIEF

Years ago when I was young and stores
were full of shoppers looking for new clothes
and gadgets sold at prices always marked down
promising to make our lives much better,
I joined them in seeking something more
and followed them in discontent and longing.
Walking with the posture of a question
mark I happened to look down and saw
what other shoppers cast aside or dropped
—some old eyeglasses and a hearing aide.
I put them on and saw in a new way
and heard that ancient brandnew Word.
That's when my questtion mark began to straighten
and become more like an exclamation!*

". . . that which we have seen and heard we proclaim also to you . . .*" (See I John 1:1-4)

"I believe . . ."

REVELATION

How I believe what I believe I do
not know. I only know I do believe
not just because of people I have known
or heard or read. There's Something More at work
in me, on me than just their deeds and words.
It is the Something More at work in that
Library our ancestors left behind
for any who with all their soul are searching
for the Word that sets life right, the Grace
that sets us free to say with confidence
and more than joyful hope: "This I believe."

"I believe in . . ."

MORE THAN A PARACHUTE

Somewhere between down and up
where the air roars by the door,
men and women jump for their lives
believing not about but in parachutes.

*"I believe in **God, the Father . . .**"*

YOU ARE WHAT YOU ARE

You are no shopping mall Santa
     with a paid for "Ho, ho, ho"
     asking what we want for Christmas.
Nor are You like abusive dads
     who find some twisted satisfaction belting
     sons and daughters who are not just so.
Nor are You merely what our hidden hopes and fears
     creatively construct with the few concepts
     we've collected in our heads across the years.
Every time we or some Moses asked
     just who You are or what You are
     all You have answered through a mystery of silence
     is "I am whatever it is, whoever it is that I am."*

You are what You are,
     regardless of what we say You are:
the unknowable that makes itself known,
     the basic mystery
     that is
that is behind, beneath, beyond all I see or know that is,
     that limits my knowledge with vastness,
     and thwarts my ego with people and with truth,
     that punctures my pride with facts,
     and finally stops my breath with time,
     that makes me so I make
     and makes me so I laugh as well as cry,

that grants me meaning beyond my knowing
and gives me peace that baffles the world,
that gives me purpose beyond human causes
and the kind of hope that is more than merely wishing,
that offers me a special fellowship of caring,
and giving me love enables me to love,
that recognizes me for who I am
and nevertheless says: "Thou."

Your ineffable Word of limits and infinity
declares through mystery the "no"
that when embraced amazingly becomes
the "yes" that transforms
       injustice into justice,
       apathy into compassion,
       greed into sharing,
       hate into love
       despair into hope
       and death into life.
And when I call You "Father,"
You let me discover I'm your much loved child,
an heir and steward of your kingdom.

*Exodus 3:14

CAN YOU IMAGINE THAT?

Can you imagine the beginning?
Not just a beginning,
not merely another beginning,
but the beginning, the first,
the only true beginning?

What power can take nothing
and from it cause all the "somethings"
that ever were and ever will be
to be set in motion?

What power can take all that was
and all that ever will be
and swallow it in an ending
that is not just an ending
but the final end?

What power can contain itself
to give its children freedom
even when it knows what chaos and pain
childish abuse of freedom brings?

What power can love enough
to refrain from doing it all
thus providing for us children

the high purpose of joining in
the completion and the transformation of creation?

What power of love is strong enough
not to rescue us from our failures
thus making growth in our wisdom possible?

What power is strong enough
to endure the suffering that comes
with having given us the freedom
that makes our loving possible?

What power of wisdom is wise enough
to appear in the simple garb
 of those who look foolish to the world?

Such power is almighty
and far beyond my comprehension.

*"I believe in God
the Father almighty, **maker** . . ."*

SILENCE SPOKE

Silence spoke the Word
and meaning became light
ordering, maneuvering, using
nothingness and chaos to build a world.

The Word made more than planets, stars, and galaxies,
even more than birds and plants and bees,
even more than matter, antimatter, and energy,
even more than yesterdays of time
and tomorrow evening's breeze,
even more than skies' illusions and all that is in the seas.

The Word made us so we make
wheels and deals and chocolate cake.

*"I believe in God . . .
maker of heaven . . ."*

3 VIEWS OF HEAVEN

One View

Heaven is more than
a sometimes now or then life experience,
or a place of life beyond all the deaths
we in this life can know or imagine.
It is a creation incomprehensible
to human critters blind to the ineffable.

Another View

"Now and then,"
He said;
"Now and then;
that is when I'll love you,
 now and then.
And we will be together
now *and* then
and you will see through new eyes
cups that are more than cups
and bread that is more than bread
—a vision beyond mere dreams
and the hope beyond your hopes.
Then, you will be transformed"
He said,
"because we are together
        . . . *now* and *then*."

Yet Another View

Now and then hope explodes
like fireworks in the dark of night
and the creation
inconceivable in the dark
is seen anew in the new light.

"I believe in God . . .
*maker of . . . **earth** . . ."*

SPECK OF DIRT AND WATER

Speck of dirt and water whirling around a spark
among millions of billions of sparks in space
within the heighth and depth of infinity.

Speck of dirt and water arrogantly called "The World!!!"
by tiny human creatures strutting on the surface
of this floating fleck of damp cosmic dust.

Speck of dirt and water, a complicated
H_2O, $E=MC_2$, DNA, 2+2, & etc.
capsule of life supporting life,
product of one being supply for another.

Speck of dirt and water, the home and inspiration
of creatures who transcend and reach beyond
to dreams of beauty, hopes for justice,
and longings for that peace
stronger than any war
and beyond all understanding.

 Speck of dirt and water,
not accidental dust
but calculated gift,
like a delicate, spherical clock
especially, thoughtfully made,
freely given as a birth day gift to us children
who use it for a ball to kick around.

"I believe in God . . .
and in Jesus Christ . . ."

PART 1
THE MESSIAH

Once inside of time
the Truth beyond all time
somehow, someway became a man,
a human like the rest of us to bring out
what in truth is really best in us
through love that goes beyond our comprehension.
The Truth beyond all time came into time
becoming one of us,
enduring all that is involved
in living in the midst
of a creation gone amuck because
we creatures had forgotten who we are.
Separated from the Truth
we tried to save ourselves
from all the fears that haunt the hearts of humans
and give rise to all the ways we distort opportunities.
And making matters worse we blame and shame
each other and ourselves and hide from Truth.
Dressing ourselves in fig leaves
made of power, selfishness and pride
we place our hope of finding meaning, peace and joy
in what our money buys
and the applause our efforts win.
Afraid, we arm ourselves with all

the weapons we can use on one another:
fear filled anger, prejudice and threat,
more and better guns and bombs and lies,
especially the lies we tell ourselves.
Once inside of time
the Truth beyond all time
somehow, someway became a man,
a human like the rest of us
to bring out what in truth
is really best in us
through love
that goes beyond our comprehension.
And we called him Messiah.

PART 2
THE ESSENCE

(to be found between the lines of Matthew 26:36-42)

"Not yet . . . . Not yet.
Look. They are asleep, so little do they understand.
You heard them arguing,
each edging for some imagined place
of importance or recognition or power.

"And what of the others?
In so short a time, how could we expect them
to translate hope in any terms other than
more food, less pain, and fewer Romans?

"And if that is the hope of the masses,
isn't it understandable
that the comfortable and secure are afraid?
They think I am out to rob them,
to take away their pleasure, power, and prestige,
more than that,
their well defined laws for justifying their lives
and their heavily defended security.

"Well, at least on this point
their perception is right even if their fear is wrong;
but then, the conflict in the temple
did not exactly soothe their anxieties.

"Father, let this cup pass from me.
It is not death that frightens me,
nor is it the public humiliation,
not even the pain.
None of that do I want,
but I could more easily accept it if only . . . . . .

if only it seemed that someone understood,
if only there were signs of at least one healthy plant;
so much seed has been scattered, and, God help me,
I cannot see a single plant that's strong.

"Dear God, to die now
in the midst of such incompleteness, such barrenness . . . .
is that what You want?

"Look at them sleeping over there.
God, You know they are going to run.
Then where will we be?
Is this what You want,
a messiah who could not even hold
the loyalty of his disciples?

"More time!
Give me more time!
Three years, even with these men, is not enough.

"Let this cup pass from me.
Nevertheless,
if my failure is what You want and need,
so be it.
I am trusting You.
I'm relying on You to make it good.
If what seems to be failure is what You want,
then, I trust that somehow it is success.
With so much unfinished and incomplete,
I can only trust that somehow
You are making this the long awaited fullness of time."

"I believe in ... Jesus Christ
His only begotten Son our Lord ..."

THE PATTERN

Issued in mid-production,
he had been around from the beginning.
He was something more and something less
than what most of us expected.

This prototype water boy became the official pattern
like no other before or since,
exposing the vanity of our loves with love.
Same as we yet so different
he revealed more than what merely is.
He lived what was meant to be,
showing us what can be
and giving us hope in what will be.

Not as the hero of the team,
not as the all-star running back
but as a water boy,
the water boy, he came and comes
offering water so alive
it more than satisfies our deepest thirst.

He uniquely came as one of us,
suffered at least as much
and probably more,
then dying as we die

went into the tomb
but did not stay.
And to this day
he haunts and hounds
like no other, with a mercy
and a call for justice
that transforms what was
into what is meant to be.

"... in Jesus Christ ... who was conceived by the Holy Spirit ..."

WORD PROBLEMS

God said the Word over and over.
God said the Word but we humans
did not understand
or did not want to.
Somehow we always missed the message,
mixed it up and messed it up.
Time and again God tried until it was painfully clear
we were so accustomed to not hearing,
saying it would never be enough.

So God said: "I will show you"
and to do that came among us
incognito as a blue collar worker.

His coming was not our idea,
and certainly not our doing.
His coming was conceived by Himself.
Through the working of His Holy Spirit
the Ineffable became a human being
—not a semi-person nor an almost god;
but the Truth that was and is and ever will be
became flesh and blood, the way and the life,
able to say with a fully human tongue: "I am."

And even though we take pride

in our replacing myth with math,
we are unable to calculate or comprehend
that Word beyond our words,
and like others, ignorant in other ways
we too must be shown,
and this takes a kind of miracle
we all too often deny is possible.

"I believe in . . . Jesus Christ . . .
who was . . . born of the virgin Mary . . ."

THERE WERE TEARS

Mary in Bethlehem
There, outside the inn
her labor ended and began.

She lay there
sweating and tired on the hay,
dreaming about the promise,
warming him with her body,
feeding him from her breasts.

She lay there
with straw in her hair
smiling in the starlight
until she looked out into the darkness
that was there.

She lay there
with him so small beside her
and wept her first mothering tears.

Mary In Jerusalem
The agony of lash and thorn and nail
throbbed the seconds s l o w l y by
because the unspeakable Word was made of flesh
and like us born to tears and pain,
but his made holy by a compassion,
the quality of which we say
goes back beyond His mother.

"I believe in . . . Jesus Christ . . .
who . . . suffered . . ."

LIFE THIS SIDE OF EDEN

When wounds are real, the child's cry
is no mere plea for more attention;
it is the sound of physical pain
or cruelty's byproduct of despair.

Beneath the sound of bathroom water running
        he hid his tears of rejection when she left.

No doctor can cure the pain that strikes
        the soul when what has been longed for,
and worked for, for so long
        is hopelessly wrecked by circumstance.

The parents' agony is more than disappointment;
        it is the undiluted agony of failure when
their teenage child spits on their love
        and sabotaging so much potential
is jailed in sullen anger of addiction.

        There is no pretense in real suffering.
To be truly human on this side of Eden
        pain is inescapable and unavoidably endured.

Into all this Jesus was born
to live and suffer
not only at the hand of Pilate.

"I believe in . . . Jesus Christ . . .
*who suffered **under Pontius Pilate** . . ."*

THE FREE MAN

He was a free man
(this local commandant)
free from moralistic hang-ups,
free from bondage to ideals,
free to meet the needs of the moment,
free to ignore regulations,
free to cut red tape such as trials.

He was a secular man
in the midst of an overly religious city
        —free.
So, once upon a time,
a small price was paid to keep the peace
and hands were washed clean—freely.

"I believe in . . . Jesus Christ . . .
*who . . . **was crucified** . . ."*

CRUCIFIXION

Who has not been to Golgatha?
The man openly lived "yes."
We locked doors and enforced "no."
He offered water.
We took blood.
With nails and wood
we did what we could.
But since then,
we have learned of other ways
to impale demanding love too freely given.
What is your favorite method?
Mine is silence and ice.
Who has not been to Golgatha?

"I believe in . . . Jesus Christ . . .
who . . . was crucified,
dead and buried . . ."

DETAILS

He was limp.
There was no life in him,
although he continued to drip blood
as we carried him from there.
Flies followed us down the hill
and bothered us wrapping his body.

The tomb at sunset
filled with a slaughter house smell
as darkness invaded the world.

His blood on our hands
mixed with our running sweat and stung
as we tried to wipe grief from our eyes.

We were sick and alone and could not sleep
in the darkness remembering the day,
remembering the flies and the blood,
remembering the smell in the tomb.

"I believe in . . . Jesus Christ . . .
who was crucified,
dead and buried . . ."

WHEN JUSTICE AND MERCY MINGLED AS ONE

Some say that terrible day was when
God's holy justice was placated
and the heavenly books
were balanced in the only way
they could be balanced
in a holy system of accounting
that could not ignore all that's wrong and horrid.

But I say it was something other, something more
than balancing of God's holy justice books
through Golgatha agony that was at work.
In mystery beyond what our best brains can grasp,
God caused justice and mercy to mingle as one,
a mind boggling act beyond mere justice
and more, much more than merely mercy.

God did more than just be Godly
when God took on all we are,
suffering through his son and as the son,
the consquences of all hell
we humans past and present have set loose.
Yet even more, God suffered even more.
In the mystery of holy time God suffered
as only parents suffer and have suffered
something worse than death.

Parents who have had to watch their child
suffer because of human injustice,
suffer because of human cruelty,
suffer because of human frailty,
suffer to death and die
know there are some things worse than mere death.

God endured that double agony,
not merely endured but willingly endured
all for the sake, in that time and space,
of working to restore what was meant to be
among ungrateful children of His creation.

It was an amazing deed of even more than love,
an act both in and far beyond our time and space
an act beyond our comprehension,
difficult to believe,
and almost impossible to follow.

"I believe in . . . Jesus Christ . . .
the third day he rose from the dead . . ."

PART 1
MORE

More than a cliche about butterflies
emerging from chrysalis shrouds.
More than the familiar songs
about multicolored flowers emerging
from the drab brown grass of winter.
More than Easter baskets can ever hold.
More than a tomb can contain much less retain.
More than resusitation of dead flesh.
More, much more, than merely more.

PART 2
THE CHALICE

It seems the once in history chalice
that held and holds life-giving drink
is destroyed time and time again
in fits of anger and of fear,
shattering in a thousand slivers
which cut to the bone all those
who try to pick up the broken pieces
to glue them back together
in some design of their own making
using their Babel tower building ingenuity
that results in chaos and futility

transforming hope into despair
until somehow
                    by the grace of God
(sometime between an awful Friday
            and a most amazing Sunday)
the shattered chalice is made ready
                    again and again
to serve the healing wine once more
with the toast: "To life! To life! *L'chiam!*"

PART 3
MORE THAN AN EASTER GIFT

Only through the eyes of faith was he seen.
The empty tomb, the folded cloth
did not convince the unconvinced.
Who of reason and common sense
could ever really believe God interviened
to raise him up from death
and bring to naught
the wisdom of all for whom
the ways of Herod, Caiaphas and Pilate
are the ways that make the most sense?
To such folk
the story was and is from fairy land
and yet one that disturbs the peace
of rulers who decide what's right
and an embarrassment (if not heresy)
for those whose life goal is to be first
and never last in their world.

Such folk did not and do not see nor want to see
the one that death could not keep in the tomb,
the one set free to transform the world.
To be able to see and believe takes more
than words from distraught women
and guilt ridden men.
It takes more than the best made arguments

to transform doubts and fears to faith and hope
and most of all to love beyond all that we love.
It takes a very specal, even holy dove
uniquely gliding into the depths
of our independent, uniquely individual hearts.

"I believe in . . . Jesus Christ . . . who . . .
was crucified, dead and buried;
the third day he rose from the dead . . ."

THE REAL THING

In a world
where wishes and dreams,
mirror tricks and illusions,
all masquerade as hope,
it is not easy to see the real thing.
It takes a divine intervention in the heart,
to heal our blindness
so we can see beyond what died
and discover there new life
made known and possible
in cross and resurrection.

By a mystery too profound to comprehend,
cross and resurrection are not two events
but one, a reality separately inseparable,
in which all that was tearing life apart
is converted to the purpose of reconciliation,
and all that was so terribly wrong
is overcome by love to be raised up in truth.
Then, what was destroyed begins to build,
and despair is born again as hope.

*"I believe in . . . Jesus Christ who . . .
ascended into heaven . . ."*

ASCENDED INTO HEAVEN

Not too long ago,
as the creation measures time,
we spoke of looking up
believing that
beyond the sky-blue dome,
beyond the moon and stars
was the place where God resides.
But Jesus and astronomers
have helped us see
there really is no "up" but only "out"
and that the place of God is not one place
and heaven not beyond the stars
but rather it is here *and* there
and *now* as well as *then*
that God is present
and where God is present
there is heaven.
There and even here
is where the Christ ascended to confront us
in the hungry, naked needy in our midst. *
It is there, by the grace of God,
we're offered life beyond mere life;
and offered the great gift
of living *now* as well as *then*
where God is present.

It is then,
when we reach out to the ones
in whom Jesus said he would reside
we find ourselves with him
ascending into heaven.

* See Matthew 25:31-46

*"I believe in . . . Jesus Christ . . . who . . . **sitteth at the right hand of God the Father Almighty . . . .**"*

AFTER THE DANCE WITH DAD

After the dance
he went home
to think about
       his date.

      So it is.
      So it is.
With Dad by the fireside
      so it is.
Will she return his love?
Or rejected will he write it off as
just another waste of holy time?

"I believe in . . . Jesus Christ . . . he shall come to judge the quick (the living')"

PART 1
THE BEGINNING OF WISDOM

The fear of the Lord is the beginning of wisdom,
and the knowledge of the Holy One is insight. Proverbs 9:10

In the prehistory wilderness there was
Something[1] hidden in the glare
of the brilliant light of sunrise.
Our ancestors strained their tearing eyes
and their hearts would race in fear
more frequently than in hope.
Separated from that ancient world of ax
and wedge and wilderness by our new
power saws and well paved subdivisions
we lost our fear and thought we had it made.
We thought we had that *Something* that
awakened fear and trembling long ago[2]
explained and declared impotent
by our sophomore introduction to psychology,
our lab notes from physics-101,
and articles we read about the big-bang.
Because we cannot comprehend or control *It*
with our brains, we ignore, doubt or deny.
Yet *that Reality* is and has been always there
(aware of *It* or not) like the ocean
is to the fish who live and move
and have their being in its depths.

Aware of *It* or not, believe it or not,
once again *It's* throwing back the covers like
a man who's overslept. Invisibly *It* invades
all we claim and think is ours or mine.
In the past some called *It* "Eloheim"
or "Adonai," or "Yahweh" or "Jehovah."
More recently we've called *It* "God" but now
that word has become only another word
used in cursing or surprise and too small
to be that awesome *What?* beyond all time
creating us and stalking us through time
with an impatient patience all its own.

1. *"I am what I am"* or *"I am who I am"* or *"I will be who/what I will be"*—Exodus 3:14

2. *". . . work out your salvation in fear and trembling."*—Philippians 2:12

PART 2
THE WAY IT WAS IN MOSES' DAY AND IN OURS

(See Exodus 1-15)
The makers of bricks for the pyramids of life
cry and cry out: "Does *the holy One* care?"
while those with profit and power live on without fear
doubting that God (if there is one) really cares or hears.

But should *The Ineffable* send someone their way,
a Moses whose words question all that they say,
they know a few tactics, some well proven tricks
such as giving no straw for the making of bricks.

It seems they're in charge (for a while anyway)
so they confidently down play the Moses-like message.
Then at last comes the day when bills must be paid
and their world falls apart in plague after plague.

PART 3
ECHOES OF AMOS TODAY

(See the Book of Amos, especially chapters 4-6)
Somewhere in the smog
where addicts have lost hope,
where children schooled in mistrust
by more parents than they can count
and fewer than they can count on,
where the abused are blamed for their pain,
where intimidation wins
and the meek lose all they inherited,
where the poor for blamed for their poverty
and everyone strives for golden parachutes,
where fears and old hates, frustration and hopelessness
motivate those with twisted intelligence to build bombs
that explode their devoted carriers into oblivion
and terrorize those who must pick up the pieces,
—where all of this and more is the usual news
Something more unerving than the angel of death
is saddling up for one more ride,
and this time *It* will not stop with the first born.

PART 4
WAITING

Waiting in our cells
that we have made
with our cell phones silenced
and focused on the latest app,
we ignore or cannot hear
if the cell phone is ringing.
They say the decision will come any day now.
Is the phone ringing
      with news?
      with decisions?
Some say it has already rung.
Some say it is ringing now.

(How else can you explain all this sorrow?)
We try to stop the news
silencing the cell phone.
But is our cell phone ringing?

PART 5
THE HOPE THAT IS OURS

(see Exodus 12)
Search the pastures for that lamb.
Send out more than one rider.
We are scared and long for the blood
that will cause what is coming to pass over.

We all want to paint our door posts,
the oppressed and oppressor alike.
But only those willing to leave for a new land,
abandon the old land and leave what is familiar behind
are given the valuable paint.

Now we wait in the evening.
The sun is going down.
We eat a supper that is stranger than usual,
but talk calmly, stealing glances at the clock
(we do not want to frighten the children
        or needlessly worry Grandma).
What is coming, is coming.

Deep down we know (perhaps are afraid)
that Israel is not determined by birth
and Passover not by blood,
and mercy not given for the mere absence of goods
nor denied by the mere presence of things.
Deep down we know that what is coming,
whatever is coming, is coming
sniffing to find whose scrapbooks are burning
and who are packing their bags
and willing to head for the wilderness trusting
whatever is coming will bring them new life.

"I believe in . . . Jesus Christ . . . who . . .
shall come to judge the . . . dead . . . ."

WHEN ALL IS SAID AND DONE

There comes a time when all is said and done,
when schedules we have made are set aside,
when what has been and what will be collide
beyond all time and space. There, memory
of what has been is held up like a sculpture
we have carved to be examined and judged
for its flaws and beauty by the only One
who really knows and truly loves us with
a love beyond our comprehension. There,
in faithful fear and trembling,
we await the verdict.

*". . . I believe in **the Holy Spirit . . .**"*

A STRANGE WIND

What blows the wind
that causes leaves to dance
between the limb and earth?

What starts the lung
inhaling breath at birth,
the fuel to cry: "I AM!"?

What causes me to care
beyond what gives rewards?

What brings strange peace
to me although the storm
still threatens all I own?

What heals my eyes
enabling me to see
what I refused to see?

A strange wind is blowing,
yet I only see leaves
twisting and swirling
until it is mine
that is caught in the whirling.
Then,
caught in the May dance of October leaves,
the fall is transformed
into a new spring.

"I believe in . . . the holy catholic church . . ."

PART 1
THE HOLY CHURCH IN THE REAL WORLD

> Out of the graveyard, into the nursery
> the blind man carries a cripple
> who sees for his sightless eyes.
> It is more than a practical bargain.
>
> Meanwhile in the crowd a couple of children
> remembering a promise lay claim to a presence[1]
> as they shine shoes and sing:
> > "Out of the wilderness
> > the white dove flew.[2]
> > In spite of hopelessness
> > the white dove knew
> > the way to happiness
> > for me and you.
> > Out of the wilderness,
> > the white dove flew."
>
> The crowd, in a hurry to get its business done,
> more often than not ignores the children
> and failing to see the difference
> > between pigeons and doves
> > curses both.

[1]Matthew 18:20 *"For where two or three are gathered in my name, there am I in the midst of them."*

PART 2
MORE THAN HERE AND NOW AND US

Just as a home is more than a house,
just as a family is more than mom, dad and the kids,
just as living involves more than now,
just as today is not independent from the past
and tomorrow is not cut loose from today,
just as a river is a constant flow
and not merely one point on the bank,
just as any place on earth is not disconnected
from all other places on earth,
just as each participates in all,
just so is the church
and that is what makes it catholic
not merely in space but also in time.

"I believe in . . . the communion of saints . . ."

LONELINESS IS AN ILLUSION

Loneliness is an illusion
—like being alone at a family reunion.
Even when I feel alone,
or in some sort of rejecting of my kin
take my plate outside to eat alone,
I am not really alone.
It is a family reunion, for Christ's sake!
Who can be alone in a family reunion?

Of course, I can live in my world of illusion
—if you want to call that living—
and shut my eyes and close my ears to what was and is.
Meanwhile, my brothers and sisters tell stories
about our ancestors and kin,
recalling what they said and did.
And somehow in the telling,
they become more than memory;
they are so present they speak still
and not antique outdated words
but words of ever renewing meaning.
My name being linked to theirs,
they claim me as their own,
even when I eat outside, alone.
When at last love transforms my pride
and I rejoin the family at the table,
I experience the mystery of being named and claimed,
and find myself,
embraced in a very real and holy communion.

*"I believe in . . . **the forgiveness of sins** . . ."*

PART 1
AN OLD MAN'S PLEA

When the crowd heard Jesus say: "Let him who is without sin cast the first stone," they went away, one by one beginning with the oldest . . . See John 8:2-11

The old man was the first to leave
Jesus scribbling in the dirt
and the woman with fear
and shame in her eyes.
He walked away,
bent, not by the years
as much as by the memories
that were always there
waiting in the shadows of his mind
to ambush his infrequent joy.

Centuries later
someone with mileage and memories
reads the old story
sighs in painful understanding:
  "In my head I believe
  God forgives me for the messes I have made.
  that God is focused on what yet can be,
  not on my screw-ups in the past.
  But where can I go, what can I do
  to finally forgive myself
  not for some harm I did to me
  but for what I said and failed to say

did and failed to do
that did damage to the ones I love?
Memories of my good intentions
gone astray in the yesterdays I can't forget
invade my memory like an army
on a never ending mission of seek out and destroy,
slaughtering joy with weapons
which reality and consequences supply.
O God, where is that death to old distortions,
that death to self that sets one truly free
from bondage to the past and sin,
the death that precedes one's new birth,
precedes new life that's really new,
the miracle of new creation
and peace beyond all understanding?
Lord have mercy. Christ have mercy.
Empower me to have mercy on myself."
Bent by a load of more than years he walks away.

PART 2
TRUE FREEDOM

She looked into her yesterday
the way some look into a mirror.
The reflection she discovered
made her turn away
in more than mere denial
of the self she saw.

At times she sought relief
in blaming, shaming and in anger
laying claim to pity for herself
because of all that in her yesterdays
had caused her fall from the ideal
that she yet claimed to be.

Then, somehow,
in a word of grace that came alive

she felt the stirring of new life within,
that with some labor pain
resulted in the miracle of birth, rebirth
and life anew that's blessed
with wisdom from her memories
yet freed from bondage
to what haunted her in yesterday.

PART 3
DIVINE INSANITY

"Don't you see?" the inmate asked.
I wanted to laugh at the crazy man
but did not dare to smile.

"It was more than a reprieve.
I hung the man,
and dying he cleared me."
I assumed he was insane
since what he said made no sense to me.

"I am free.
I am free,"
he sang to me.

But anyone could see
he was not really free;
he was an inmate in this special place.

With laughter in his eyes he looked at me
and said he saw I did not see
that it was true that he was free.

"It was more than a reprieve.
I hung the man and dying he cleared me.
Here. Have some bread.
The man I hanged left it behind.
It heals whatever ails you."

He offered just a crumb, no bigger than a wafer
and a special cup of more than wine to drink.
And what was in it went beyond my head
        and to my heart.
Then he laughed his laugh
and sang his song
about it being more than a reprieve
when he saw it happen once again
        —a shameful wounded, broken something
        I had learned to live with through denial
        was made strangely clean and whole.

And so I joined this man
in his divine insanity
that sets free in us a strange joy
that even here and with our past
gives us the freedom to laugh and dance.

"I believe in . . . the resurrection of the body and the life everlasting."

PART 1
MORE THAN JUST ENOUGH

Some say that when the whistle blows the game
comes to an end. Some say the whistle only
means another quarter has begun.
Some say that when the whistle blows it really
means the Umpire of all umpires will
announce who gets the trophies
and who catches hell for all of what is said to be
beyond all time and all we know of space.
All of this and more is what some say
in their attempt to say it's in God's hands.

Others say that there is something more;
that trusting God (the one beyond all gods)
is like John says*—it's more than just enough.
They say God's miracle and mystery of grace
transforms us all with peace and joy
beyond imagination, even beyond the grave.

* John 3:16-17 *For God so loved the world that he gave his only Son, that whoever believes in him should not perish but have eternal life. For God sent the Son into the world, not to condemn the world, but that the world might be saved through him.*

PART 2
MORE THAN MORE

Something wrong in Granddad's head transformed
his kindness into anger frightening all
who tried to reach him, even our Grandma.
He lost his smile the same place he mislaid
the memories and the names of all he loved.

Don't speak to me of life beyond the grave
continuing our lives the way they are
and in the same breath tell me: "God is love."
Granddad, forever trapped in his dementia?
Lives and psyches cruelly twisted by
distorted genes or generations of
abuse trapped in what was beyond their choice?

I need to hear the message in Paul's words
that speak of being raised to a new life,
as different as the plant is from its seed.*
Pray not that those who die continue on.
Pray for resurrection to new life,
and by the grace of God the gift
of more, much more than merely more.

*See I Corinthians 15

". . . Amen."

THE TREE

There it is,
bigger than it was last time.
Remember when we walked here holding hands?
We said it then, but saying it seemed so small
we carved it on the tree to say: "It's true."
We've come and gone a thousand times
to see the tree and what was carved.
And when we do,
each time we do,
we know it is more than true.
"There it is,"
      we say again,
"bigger, more true than it was the last time."

Comments about Creeds in General and the Apostles' Creed in Particular

CREEDS ARE STUMBLING BLOCKS FOR SOME

FOR MANY OF US Christians, creeds are stumbling blocks we view as outdated and irrelevant. If the creed does not immediately make sense to us, we tend to view it as an antique that is no longer useful or relevant. If the content of the creed appears on the surface to be at odds with our perception of reality, we tend to discard it as being nothing more than a lifeless relic from the past that only the uneducated and unthinking can affirm with integrity.

We can so value our individual personal experiences as the primary verification of truth that we devalue wisdom of others that we do not understand and especially wisdom from those who lived before our time. It is not unusual for us to deal with their statements with impatience and self-centeredness, responding: "Since it does not make sense to me I am justified in ignoring it as irrelevant religious gibberish." Confident in our judgment, we exempt ourselves from the effort of trying to understand what our ancestors in the faith meant and the wisdom with which they addressed their situation and concerns.

This attitude was certainly mine when I entered seminary in the late 1950's. I was in such an intense reaction against anti-intellectual, literalistic Christian fundamentalism, I not only thought the ancient creeds were irrelevant, I had serious doubts about the Christian faith in general. My reason for going to seminary was more of a quest to discover some sort of hope that would make life worth living than it was the act of one committed to the Gospel. As I stated in the first poem in this collection, I viewed statements such as "The Apostles Creed" like "out of style eyeglasses with an almost run-down hearing aid" (the kind of glasses with a bulky hearing aide built into the ear piece of the frame) that the elderly used some decades ago.

With the help of teachers and scholars, faithful pilgrims and insightful writers, my appreciation of not only The Apostles' Creed but the rich wisdom of Christian thinkers from the past continues to mature and my debt to them increases.

So, how do I now view creeds of the Christian faith? Why are they important? Much, if not most, of what I will be saying draws heavily on the way William Barclay addressed this question in the introduction to his book *The Apostles' Creed* (published by Westminster John Knox Press) and the introduction to *Creeds Of The Church* edited by John Leith (published by Anchor Books).

CREEDS ARE IMPORTANT
FOR THE COMMUNITY OF FAITH

While being a Christian is a personal experience, it is not a private one. Love of God and love of neighbor which are at the heart of living as Christ lived takes us beyond the confines of privacy. We humans are more interdependent than we are independent (even though many in our society try to ignore or deny this truth). We have been created in community for community. One way to view the problem of sin presented in the Bible is as the breakdown of community—a distortion of being in community with God and with others.

For there to be community there must be communication. We humans have been created to talk with one another and this requires us to develop concepts that make communication possible. In addition to the mundane matters of daily living, we also share with one another what gives our lives meaning and hope. The need and importance of doing this is somewhat reflected in Jesus' command that his followers share the Gospel with the whole world (Matthew 28:19). The Book of Acts and the writings of Paul demonstrate that the Gospel is to be expressed in words as well as deeds. The Gospel is not merely a matter of feelings, regardless of how heartfelt one's faith is, and living the life of faith requires words as well as deeds.

Brief summary statements of identity and purpose are helpful—not only for religions but also other organizations. "What is your purpose statement?" a business consultant asked the owner. Such statements help us stay focused on our identity and purpose. Within the text of the Old and New Testaments there are a variety of summary statememts (for example, see Deuteronomy 6:4–5, Romans 1:3–4, Philippians 2:6–11 and others).

The early Christian community discovered they needed brief summary statements of the Gospel to maintain consistency in what was being proclaimed and taught by various followers of Christ as well as to use as summary statements in teaching the Gospel to others. These statements helped keep what was being proclaimed consistent with the Gospel revealed in Jesus Christ.

In some of the writings from the 2nd or early 3rd century we are able to identify statements that are the beginning of what centuries later came to be known as "The Apostles' Creed." "The date and place of origin of the present form of the Apostles' Creed cannot be fixed with precision. There is considerable evidence for a date in the late sixth or seventh century somewhere in southwest France."[1] Although the apostles did not write this creed, the Church (especially in the West) has been convinced that this creed expresses in summary form the faith of the apostles. A legend developed that this creed was actually written by the Apostles on the tenth day after the Ascension under the inspiration of the Holy Spirit.[2]

FULL APPRECIATION OF
THE CREEDS REQUIRES STUDY.

It is understandable that the creeds are misunderstood today because the words and concepts used belong to the era in which the creeds were written. These statements address (both explicitly and implicitly) the concerns, conflicts and challenges of those times. Full appreciation of each creed requires some study in order to understand the concerns being addressed by the creed and to discern the meaning originally intended.

This is certainly true of The Apostles' Creed. In the early years of Christianity (and in each century since then) there have been some Christians who denied the humanity of Jesus because they were convinced the material world (including the human body) is evil and that only the spirit is good. Believing this they could not believe Jesus, the Christ, could be a human being who was born and suffered and died. They believed Jesus was pure spirit only masquerading as a human being. Because they believed the

1 *Creeds Of The Church*, page 24
2 *Creeds Of The Church*, page 22.

world was evil and they believed an evil deity created the world, for them the Gospel was that the good God came in Jesus pretending to be human in order to rescue the spirits of people from the evil world. A significant factor in the development of what eventually evolved into The Apostles' Creed was the early Church saying "No!" to such mistaken notions by declaring the important basic beliefs of true followers of Jesus Christ.

It takes more than hurriedly reading the creed from the perspective of 21st century Western culture for one to begin to appreciate (much less embrace) the wisdom and profound insights the creed points toward. Many of the issues and concerns facing the early Church when The Apostles' Creed was being formed are either no longer our issues and concerns or those concerns are now expressed in very different terms. However, the truth and wisdom of The Apostles' Creed remain valid; but it does take some study to adequately understand the wisdom the creed points toward and the errors this creed attempted to set straight.

Although the distortions of the Gospel that the early Church faced are expressed differently today, many of those distortions continue to confront and challenge people who call themselves Christians. The old distortions that are still with us are merely dressed in different clothes. The creeds were developed to be a resource for helping the faithful stay on course and the creeds continue to offer wise guidance. The challenge for us in each generation is to understand the creeds from the past so that we are able to draw on the wisdom within the words written in another era that point toward the ever relevant reality of the Gospel.

To add to the problem of understanding, the meaning of words change from century to century. In our era the meaning of some words change decade to decade (for example: the definition of "gay" in 1959 and "gay" in 1969). The words first used in The Apostles's Creed are words of almost 2,000 years ago in a pre-scientific, pre-enlightenment era within the culture of the middle-east (not the 21st century in the places where most of us live).

Because it takes effort to appropriately appreciate the ancient creeds, many people are tempted to store them in a closet or dusty basement with other handed down antiques that are assumed to be no longer relevant or useful. When we do this, we lose touch with part of our Christian heritage, a major resource for living the life of faith.

THERE IS MORE TO THE GOSPEL THAN CREEDS CAN CONTAIN.

As important as creeds such as The Apostles's Creed are to the Community of Faith known as the Church, no creed is a complete and adequate expression of the Gospel. The most a creed can do is point toward the reality of the Gospel. The Gospel is more than words can ever capture. Human concepts are finally inadequate for fully expressing the Truth of God.

Being a faithful follower of Christ is not a matter of merely reciting a creed such as The Apostles's Creed as though that act earned that person some sort of passing grade from God. Being a Christian, a follower of Christ, has do to do with a view of life, an attitude toward life, a set of values and priorities that shape a way of living. Believing *in* God as Father, Son and Holy Spirit is more, much more, than merely having certain beliefs *about* God.

The experience of God's grace and living in faithful response to God's grace is what the creed points toward. Reciting the creed is a way of remembering who we are and who we are called to be. It is a declaration, a special reminder of God's grace and the promises of the Gospel. It is God's grace and the promises of the Gospel that give hope and empower living—not the words we use to remind ourselves.

Being a follower of Christ is more than merely being "a spiritual person" (a phrase that can mean whatever the individual chooses it to mean). A primary purpose of the creeds is to provide a type of norm or standard or touchstone that will help one avoid the perils of subjectivism. As William Barclay pointed out, a creed defines faith so that "Christianity cannot evaporate in a vague and nebulous feeling or glow." "A creed is necessary simply that a (person) may test (his/her) own faith and thought by the faith and thought of the universal Church."[3]

This is not to say a creed is intended to be a sort of written or spoken test to decide who will be allowed into heaven and who will be sent to hell. God is concerned about much more than religious declarations. As Jesus said in the Sermon on the Mount: "Not every one who says to me, 'Lord, Lord' shall enter the kingdom of heaven, but he who does the will of my father."[4]

3 *THE APOSTLES' CREED* by William Barclay, page 6

4 Matthew 7:21, also see Matthew 25:31–46

THERE ARE MANY CREEDS OR AFFIRMATIONS USED BY CHRISTIANS IN WORHIP.

"The Apostles Creed" is not the only creed adopted and used by various organized groups of Christians. For example, just within my heritage there are several creeds printed in the 1989 edition of *The United Methodist Hymnal*: "The Nicene Creed," "The Apostles' Creed, Traditional Verson," "The Apostles' Creed, Ecumenical Version," "A Statement of Faith of The United Church of Canada," "A Statement of Faith of The Korean Methodist Church" and "A Modern Affirmation." Also listed are affirmations from the New Testament letters of Paul: "Affirmation From Romans 8:35 & 37–39," "Affirmation From I Corinthians 12:1–6 And Colossians 1:15–20" and "Affirmation From I Timothy 2:5–6, 1:15, 3:16." Each of these affirmations help members of the community of faith remember whose they are and who they are.

THERE ARE SEVERAL USES MADE OF THE CREEDS AND AFFIRMATIONS

Our understanding of who we are as Christians is enriched by the wisdom contained and pointed toward in the creeds. Across the centuries creeds have helped shape and been embraced by faithful women and men. The creeds that have been embraced and endorsed by the community of faith (including The Apostles' Creed) were and are important to the Church in the following ways:

1. a resource for keeping the Church's preaching on course,

2. a resource giving guidance and consistency to the nurturing work of Christian teaching,

3. an affirmation to be made at baptism verifying that baptism is appropriate,

4. a resource for helping individuals discern whether or not their personal faith or spiritual experience is consistent with the Gospel as revealed in Christ, made known to us through the Bible and handed down through the Church century after century,

5. in the face of challenges and conflicts of belief, a brief resource to help keep the community consistent with what the Scriptures and the universal (catholic) Church has proclaimed.

6. In worship the reciting of the creed or affirmation of faith can be an almost mystical experience not only uniting us with those around us but also with Christians around the planet and across the ages in declaring what is at the center of life and the center of our lives. It is not the words but the reality, the truth the words point toward that bind us with one another in the sanctuary, around the planet and across the centuries.

Each of these creeds or affirmations is not a check list of *beliefs about* God, Christ, the Holy Spirit and the Church. Each in its own way and style is a reminder, a declaration of who we are and whose we are. They are statements that point to what we *believe in.*

Further Reading

The Apostles' Creed by William Barclay published by Westminister John Knox Press is a helpful introduction to The Apostles' Creed and each chapter contains extensive Scriptural and historal background information related to the phrase that chapter explains.

A History Of Christian Thought, Vol. I by Justo L Gonzales published by Abingdon Press is a helpful book for those interested in an in depth explanation of the development of Christian theology. Pages 151–154 focus on The Apostles' Creed.

The Story Of Christianity, Vol. I by Justo L Gonzales published by Abingdon Press is a readable and well researched history of Christianity. Pages 62–66 focus on The Apostles' Creed.

Creeds Of The Churches Leith, John H. (editor) published by Anchor Books contains a clear introduction regarding the uses of the creeds and background material related to the development of what we call The Apostles' Creed, especially pages 1–26.

The Faith Once Given by George Ricker is published by The Westminster Press and contains a brief readable explanation of the phrases in The Apostles' Creed.

I Believe The Christian Creed by Helmut Thielicke (translated by John W. Doberstein and H. George Anderson and published by Fortress Press) is a collection of readable and profound sermons dealing with the meaning of each phrase of The Apostles' Creed.

About the Author

JIM MAYFIELD HAS BEEN writing poetry for most of his adult life. Some years ago an earlier verision of this volume of poetry was used in a course taught at the Episcopal Seminary Of The Southwest. Across the years he has privately published 5 volumes of poetry to share with friends and has written approximately 40 lyrics with music composed by Kay Rivers Kidd. From 1962 until 1979 he wrote material for youth and adult workers with youth that was regularly published by The United Methdodist Church.

Before retiring Jim was a United Methodist pastor for more than four decades. Throughout his ministry he has sought to understand the life experiences faced by members of his congregations and to develop ministries relevant to them and to the circumstances of the communities in which he lived.

His experiences beyond the local church have run the gamut from laborer in oil exploration, to working with poverty youth while in seminary, to being involved in developing one of the first War On Poverty projects in South Texas (a successful education program enabling adults to move themselves and their families out of poverty). In Austin, Texas, for several years at Austin Presbyterian Theological Seminary he taught one of the courses required for ordination in The United Methodist Church. He also served on the Deans Advisory Board for Perkins School of Theology at SMU and served a term on the Board of Trustees of Houston Tillotson Universiry. He served 3 terms as president of the Austin Area Interreligious Ministries and was involved in leading that interreligious community in its response to 9-11-2001. For his leadership he was given the Hope Award. In 1999 he served as Chaplain of the Senate of The State of Texas, and was honored by the Senate when he retired. He held a variety offices in the Southwest Texas Conference of The United Methodist Church (now the Rio Texas Conference). The one that gave him the greatest sense of satisfaction was being elected by the clergy of the conference to serve as chairman of the Order of Elders.

Although he officially retired as a United Methodist pastor in June, 2006, he continued to be active as an ordained minister. For four years he served as a facilitator for the Texas Methodist Foundation's Institute For Clergy And Congregational Excellence, led seminars for pastors, served as interim pastor for 2 congregations, served as coach for individual pastors, led Opposite Strengths seminars, spoke and taught in churches, continued writing poems and lyrics for hymns and had two other books published: AMAZING GRACE IN THE MIDST OF GRIEF and THE SERMON ON THE MOUNT—A PERSONAL ENCOUNTER WITH THE WISDOM OF JESUS.

He holds degrees from The University Of Texas (B.A.), S.M.U. Perkins School of Theology (M.Div.) and T.C.U. Brite Divinity School (D.Min.). He was also given an honorary Doctor of Divinity degree from Huston-Tillotson University.

Jim married Rita Browning of Houston, Texas following his graduation from seminary. They have two children and five granddaughters.

www.ingramcontent.com/pod-product-compliance
Lightning Source LLC
LaVergne TN
LVHW051709080426
835511LV00017B/2810